CROCODILES

By Steve Parker
Illustrated by Steve Roberts

Miles Kelly
PUBLISHING

First published in 2002 by
Miles Kelly Publishing Ltd
Bardfield Centre,
Great Bardfield,
Essex, CM7 4SL

2 4 6 8 10 9 7 5 3 1

Editorial Director: Paula Borton
Art Director: Clare Sleven
Project Editor: Belinda Gallagher
Assistant Editors: Nicola Jessop, Nicola Sail
Designer: HERRING BONE DESIGN
Artwork Commissioning: Lesley Cartlidge
Indexer: Jane Parker

ISBN 1-84236-121-X

Printed in Hong Kong

www.mileskelly.net
info@mileskelly.net

British Library Cataloguing-in-Publication Data
A catalogue record for this book is available
from the British Library

Contents

Crocodile facts

- The saltwater crocodile grows to 7 metres long and more than 1 tonne in weight.
- It lives in South and East Asia and Northern Australia.

The **SALTWATER CROCODILE** is the biggest reptile in the world. It is far larger than any snake, lizard, turtle or tortoise. In fact, it is powerful enough to catch all kinds of prey, from small fish to large deer — even animals as big as you!

The saltwater crocodile has two keels along its tail, which are rows of tall scales.

All crocodiles and alligators have five toes on each front foot, and four toes on each back foot.

Saltwater crocodiles live in swamps, rivers and lakes. They are fierce and dangerous, especially if they are surprised or cornered. They are true 'man-eaters' and have killed many people over the years.

Seaside croc!

The saltwater crocodile gets its name because it lives in rivers and lakes, but it can also swim out to sea. Other crocodiles and alligators hate salty water!

Muggers steal fish!

Crocodile facts

- The mugger grows up to 4 metres in length.
- It lives in the Indian region.

The **MUGGER** is a strong, powerful crocodile that likes any kind of fresh water. It even hides in man-made ditches and canals. In big lakes, it follows fishing boats and then steals the fish from the nets! The mugger's jaws and teeth are strong enough to crush a turtle's shell, or drag a water buffalo under the surface so that it drowns.

A young mugger has dark stripes across its body and tail. These fade as it gets older.

Crocodiles move on land in three ways. They 'gallop' with the body off the ground, they 'waddle' with legs out to the sides, and they 'wriggle' like a snake, sliding along on the belly.

Walk like a croc

Try walking like a crocodile, with your arms and legs on the floor beneath your body. Move one arm forward, followed by the opposite leg.

Like all crocodiles and alligators, the mugger has a body armour of thick, tough scales. These scales are biggest on the back and tail.

3 Some crocodiles are small

Crocodile facts

- The dwarf crocodile is 1.5 to 2 metres in length.
- It lives in lakes, marshes and swamps in West Africa.

The **DWARF CROCODILE** is one of the smallest crocodiles. It is so little, that one frog is a big feast! So is a fish, a crayfish or a baby water bird. Unlike most crocodiles, the dwarf crocodile does not like to sit in the sun. It hides among plants by day and comes out to hunt at night.

Swish that tail!

Hold your hand on its edge in water, and swish it to and fro. This is how a crocodile uses its tail to swim. A flat hand has less power.

The dwarf crocodile may be small, but it is very well protected. It has lots of thick scales all over its body – even on its eyelids.

The dwarf crocodile is also called the short-snouted crocodile, because its nose and jaws are not very long.

Alligators are good mothers!

Alligator facts

- The American alligator grows to about 5 metres long.
- It lives in North America in swamps, rivers and lakes.

The female **AMERICAN ALLIGATOR** is a caring mother. She makes a huge pile of mud and plants, lays her 40 to 50 eggs inside, and guards them well. When the babies are ready to hatch, they squeak inside their egg shells. Their mother carefully digs them out.

The female alligator carefully pulls each egg from the nest so that the baby can break out of its egg shell.

The nest mound is like a compost heap. As the plants rot, they make heat that keeps the eggs warm.

The baby alligator inside the egg is about 22 centimetres long. After it hatches, its first meal will probably be a water insect or baby fish.

Caring mums!

With nearly all crocodiles and alligators, the female is a caring mother. She guards her eggs and babies fiercely.

5 Crocodiles always have new teeth!

Caiman facts

- The black caiman may grow to 6 metres long.
- It lives in rivers and swamps in the Amazon region of South America.

Like other crocodiles and alligators, the **BLACK CAIMAN** grows a new tooth almost every week. The old teeth get worn, chipped and broken, and fall out one by one. Each time, a new tooth grows from inside the jaw to replace the lost one. A crocodile is never toothless!

Caimans are a type of alligator. There are five different kinds of caiman and they live only in Central and South America.

Dino-crocs!

Crocodiles were around before the dinosaurs, over 200 million years ago. Some were a gigantic 15 metres long!

Black caimans are not all black. They have patterns of white spots, and grey and yellow patches, on a brown or black background.

The black caiman is the biggest hunting animal in South America. It eats large fish, turtles, water snakes, deer, and pig-like animals called tapirs. It even eats smaller kinds of caimans.

Crocodiles like to lie in wait!

Crocodile facts

- The American crocodile sometimes grows longer than 6 metres.
- It lives in southern North America to northern South America.

The **AMERICAN CROCODILE** spends most of its time doing nothing. It lies on the riverbank or floats in the water. This is part of its clever hunting method. Animals wander past, stop to drink, and SNAP! They get dragged into the water and torn to pieces!

As a crocodile floats in water, perfectly still, it looks like a harmless old log. Its eyes and ears are above the surface, as is its nose, so that it can breathe. The crocodile looks and listens, waiting for its next meal.

Crocodiles are cold-blooded, like other reptiles such as snakes and lizards. If the weather is cool, they can only move very slowly. After they warm up their bodies by lying in the sun, they can run as fast as you!

Longer = older!

Crocodiles live to a great age – if they stay out of trouble. The older they are, the longer they grow. Some are over 100 years of age!

American crocodiles sometimes gather in groups. They come together where there is lots of food. The feast might be a shoal of fish, or a group of pig-like animals called peccaries, which have drowned in a flood.

Hunting underwater

The **GHARIAL** breathes air into its lungs, like other crocodiles. But it can hold its breath and stay underwater for a long time — more than half an hour. Gharials can also hunt underwater, and even eat their prey there.

Gharials spend a lot of time in the water, chasing fish. They do not move about on land as much as other crocodiles.

Like all crocodiles, the gharial has flaps of skin called webs, between its toes. These help to push through the water when swimming.

To swim fast, crocodiles swish their tails and steer with their feet. They can also swim slowly by just paddling with their feet.

Bumpy nose!

The male gharial has a lump on the front of its nose, at the tip. The female gharial does not.

The gharial's long snout is very thin. It has lots of small, pointed teeth — perfect for catching slippery fish.

Sleeping reptiles

Alligator facts

• The Chinese alligator is one of the smallest of the crocodile group – less than 2 metres long.
• It lives in only a few areas of China.

Crocodiles do not rush about. They are still for much of the time, as they soak up the sun and watch for prey. If the weather is cold crocodiles have to lie still, because they are too cool to move. The **CHINESE ALLIGATOR** is still all winter. It sleeps in a cave or burrow and wakes up in the warmth of spring.

Rarest of all!

Chinese alligators are rare. They live in only a few areas of the lower reaches in the Chang-Jiang (Yangtze) River.

The Chinese alligator lives mainly in this pink shaded area

CHINA

The winter sleep of the Chinese alligator is called dormancy. It lasts from about October to March. When the alligator wakes up, it is very hungry!

The teeth of the Chinese alligator are suited to crushing tough food. It eats river snails, clams, freshwater crabs and other hard-shelled creatures.

Crocodiles are not fussy

Caiman facts

- The common caiman lives in many parts of Central and South America.
- It rarely grows longer than 3 metres.

The **COMMON CAIMAN** likes any fresh water, from natural lakes and rivers, to man-made canals, ditches, and the reservoirs which collect behind dams. It even lies in the water troughs put out for farm animals. When they come for a drink – SNAP!

The common caiman has a bony ridge in front of each eye. It looks as if it is wearing glasses. This why sometimes it is called the spectacled caiman.

Caimans catch fish, water birds and river snails. They even eat piranhas – fierce fish with sharp teeth.

The common caiman has the strongest body armour of almost any crocodile. Each piece is as thick and tough as the heel of a boot.

On the move

Common caimans prefer swampy areas, but will move around to live almost anywhere. They have even been known to survive in dry grasslands.

Crocodile facts

- The Nile crocodile can reach almost 6 metres in length.
- It lives in many parts of Africa.

There are 23 kinds of crocodiles, alligators and caimans. One of the most dangerous is the **NILE CROCODILE**. Each year it kills more people in Africa than lions do! Luckily, after a big meal, a crocodile can last for a month or two before it's hungry again.

The Nile crocodile waits in the muddy water, for a thirsty animal to come and drink.

When a crocodile relaxes with its mouth wide open, birds such as *spur-winged plovers* pick its teeth clean – and get their own meal.

Many crocodiles swallow stones, to make themselves heavier. Then they can float unseen, just below the surface, right up to their prey.

Croc farms

Well-fed crocodiles living on farms grow almost twice as fast as those in the wild.

Index

BB10/02